"MYTHOPŒIKON"

Fantasies   Monsters   Nightmares   Daydreams

The paintings, book-jacket illustrations and record-sleeve designs of

Patrick Woodroffe

With a commentary by the artist

Copyright © 1976 by Patrick Woodroffe
Originally published by Dragon's World
Limpsfield and London
All rights reserved
including the right of reproduction
in whole or in part in any form
A Fireside Book
Published by Simon and Schuster
A Division of Gulf & Western Corporation
Simon & Schuster Building
Rockefeller Center
1230 Avenue of the Americas
New York, New York 10020

ISBN 0-671-22910-9
ISBN 0-671-22932-X Pbk.
Library of Congress Catalog Number 77-76740
Produced and designed by Patrick Woodroffe
Manufactured in Great Britain (First Printing)
Reprinted in Japan by Dai Nippon Printing Co., Ltd.

MYTHOPŒIKON

There are two worlds for every man. He has his day to day world of quiet routine in unpredictable nature—a leisurely tightrope walk over a cataract of tragedy. The rope's end—death—hangs in the air like a short branch. And any step of the way he may slip, fall and perish in real agonies;

real beasts wait to devour him.

But as he walks, he may close his eyes and retreat into a world enclosed within the walls of his skull, a world confined to tiny electric pathways between billions of minute brain cells.

Fantastic art is the cartography of this

nowhere-land. And we may see familiar places there—familiar faces too. We all know this nowhere—the joy we feel is the joy of recognition, of rediscovery.

So let us embark for the gilded horizons of the mind. Let us set foot on strange islands, study the abundant flora and fauna, meet the strange and fabulous people who live there. And if our ship should plunge over the lip of the ocean and fall into bottomless space—no matter—there is plenty there to please us too.

Previous pages: Cover Art for "The Ship of Ishtar"
by A. Merritt, published by Avon Books, U.S.A.
Acrylic gouache, ink and crayon.

PATRICK WOODROFFE
Delineavit

CONTENTS:

Section

1940   Born in Halifax, Yorkshire
1964   Graduated in French and German at Leeds University
1966   Small exhibition of drawings at the ICA
1972   Abandoned intermittent teaching in Cornwall to become a free lance illustrator. Successful exhibition at the Covent Garden Gallery in London
1976   Exhibition at Mel Calman's gallery "The Workshop" in London

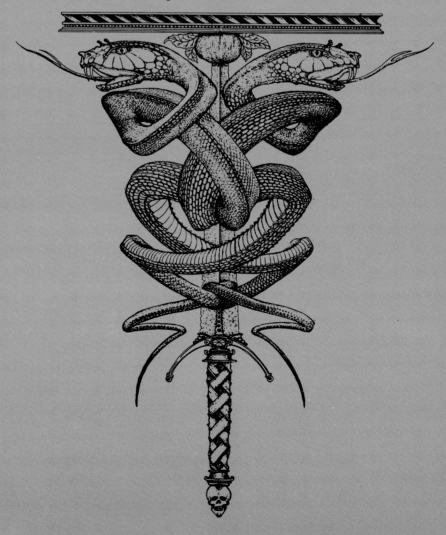

Above: THE FIDDLER'S BRIDE. Oil on canvas.

This painting was based largely on the second movement of Mahler's 4th Symphony, a movement sub-titled 'Death takes the Fiddle', in which strange violin notes evoke the old German theme of Death and the Maiden. In a book I had seen some illustrated and rhyming arithmetic lessons, in which a child, having trouble with her sums, is helped by a mysterious little gnome. The rhyme ran: "All at once a funny man was standing by her side.." And to this I added: "...the Fiddler's Bride." And so we have the bride who is betrothed to Death.

Section One:
EARLY INFLUENCES

It was not until I was at least twenty-five that I came to understand what painting really meant for me. By then I had become familiar with the work of Salvador Dali, the Viennese school of 'fantastic realism', and above all with the work of Dutch and Flemish so-called 'primitives' of the Middle Ages and Renaissance.

I suddenly knew that painting could achieve something that no camera could ever achieve, that for me art was to be a means by which a new world could be revealed, a world seen only within the mind.

Above: NOAH'S ARK II. Pen and ink. France 1963.

CONFLICT. Pen and ink. Falmouth 1965.

 1 There is a gentle conflict in the world of fish.
 2 Natural conflict does not destroy.
 3 The meadow hides a miraculous battle.
 4 It seems a pity to destroy anything whatsoever.
 5 The wars of men are sick.
 6 C'est magnifique—la guerre!
 7 —And death triumphs—innocents stand by—.
 8 But from death emerges sweetness.
 9 The devil weeps to be redeemed.
10 And it is granted.

7

My first attempts reflected the powerful influences of those who had gone before. I began by unashamedly imitating Dali, weighed down by memories of his powerful images, unable to escape from his monumental shadow.

Gradually I started to invent for myself, to comment in my own words on the beauties and follies around me. While in France studying for my degree, I produced a number of drawings on various themes of my own. Later, back in England, I followed the first drawings with a series entitled *Conflict*, which attempted to understand the painful necessity of death and destruction. These drawings and those done in France were exhibited at the Institute of Contemporary Arts in 1966.

Above: ALPENMADONNA. Oil on canvas.

    While spending a year in France as a languages assistant, I often went up into the Vosges Mountains and viewed the Alps from afar; and below me there would be the Rhine valley shrouded in haze. This is the setting for my madonna; and here as in *Conflict 10* the octopus emerges as a symbol of love and reassurance.

Below: SOUL TAKING FLIGHT. Oil on wood.

    Ideas slowly began to flow. The music of Gustav Mahler and Anton Bruckner—those ecstatic and inexorable symphonies—flashed new images in my mind. The instruments of the orchestra spoke with the voices of birds, fish, and fabulous beasts.

Below: ODE TO JOY. Oil, copper, glass on wood.

    My wife Jean was pregnant for the first time when I painted this one. The many-handed god smiling down on the nativity is Aton of ancient Egypt, who was often represented as a disc surrounded by tiny hands. The title is that of Schiller's poem, set by Beethoven in his 9th Symphony.

    The technique combines flat painting in oils with other materials. Using tin tacks, copper wire, nails, and glass beads made over a bunsen burner, I tried to make a new, more sumptuous setting in which to place my images. Since then I have come to prefer an even, regular surface on a painting; the illusion rather than the reality of three dimensions.

Above: POSEIDON'S CHILDREN. Oil, copper and glass on wood.

Here I have used fishes as symbols of love and vitality. And the snail, one of the most successful of all species, yet so vulnerable and fragile, lives on a plain of lowly calm and innocence which I have always envied. The big round face represents Poseidon, god of the sea.

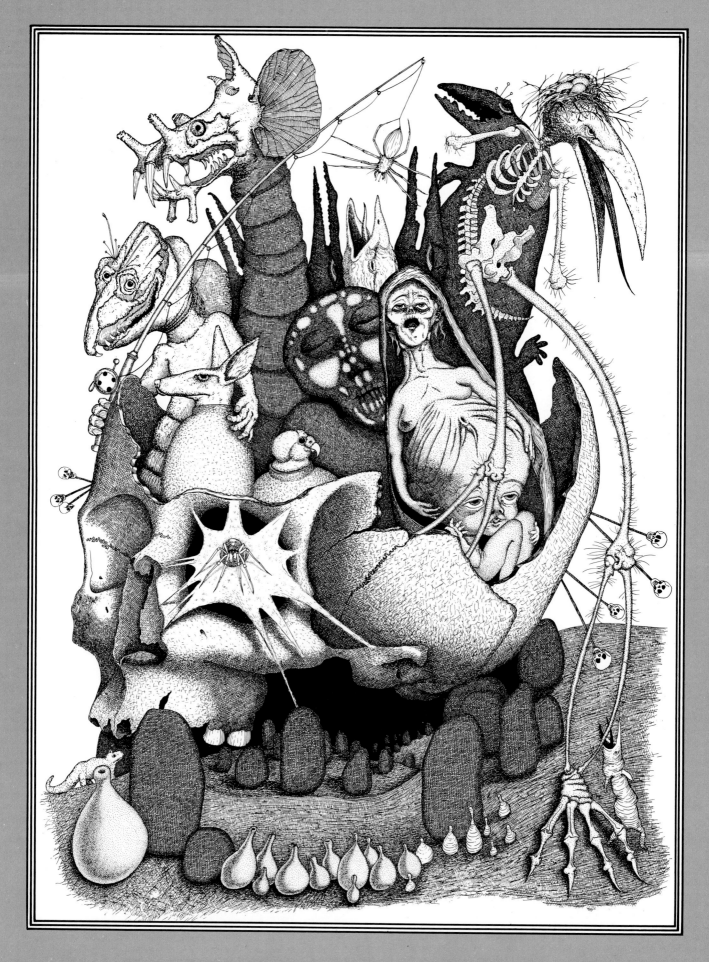

Above: DIS IS THE PERSONIFICATION OF DEATH, NEGATION AND DESTRUCTION. Rapidograph.

Drawing can sometimes be used as a sort of ceremonial exorcism by which our fear may be neutralised.

Above: PERHAPS WE MAY STILL BE ABLE TO RESCUE THEM. Rapidograph. (In the collection of Gordon Rattray-Taylor).

I took this line from an unpublished story I wrote at this time. The foolish, the misled, and their brutalities.

Above right: THE FOOL'S CAP. Rapidograph. (In the collection of Anthony Fry).

The fool is the unknown warrior, the anonymous killer, who does as he is told no matter what it may be. Underneath the armour and the mask he is still a child, and one day he will wake up in soiled sheets and cry for his mother.

Right: THE STAR CHILD. Rapidograph. (In the collection of Nick Hobson).

The title comes from Oscar Wilde's lovely story. Here the child is my son Danny—a visitor from outer space. He is alone and naked in a world full of enemies and friends, unable to distinguish one from the other. This is theme which I took up again later in the series of drawings *The Child-Stealers*, and still later in the triptych *The Thousand-Year Roundabout.*

I was introduced to the Rapidograph pen by Richard Humphrey, the painter, and used it enthusiastically for several years. With this ingenious instrument, now commonplace, pen and ink is a remarkably easy medium, but I have since come to appreciate that the uniform thickness of line is not as expressive as the swelling line of the traditional mapping pen or the subtle effects obtainable on an etching plate.

And so back to oils and canvas. I had seen the remarkable work of Richard Humphrey in London, and his fertile imagination and incredible skill urged me to add my voice to his in a song of praise to the glory of Nature!

I wanted to emulate the wide and busy canvases of Hieronymus Bosch, to paint pictures that could be read like books, explored like new worlds. Only by filling the entire surface could I satisfy my urge to invent; and only when the picture was full could I say that it was finished. I wanted to express the oneness of Nature, the vibrant dynamism which constantly ebbs and flows through matter.

THE BIRTH OF ANIMATED NATURE. Oil on canvas, 864 mm x 864 mm. 1965. (Reproduced by permission of John Enders).

The living world springs from the living soil. The mountains tremble, begin to breathe. A heart beats under the crust of the Earth. You cannot tell where the rocks end and the roots begin, where the leaf stops and the flesh takes over. The whole joyful crowd swims in the wind. Ships, space-craft, gas balloons—not inventions but discoveries—are as much a part of Nature as anything else. And the genius of Daedalus must use the feathers of other flying things to make his death-escaping wings.

Again the octopus has a part to play; the tentacles seek us out in the depths of the Earth and draw us up and back. The fish are wondrous moving things left high and dry by an exceedingly sudden ebb-tide! And the summit of this new mountain is already spread with snow, and small satellites spring off and float away silently into space.

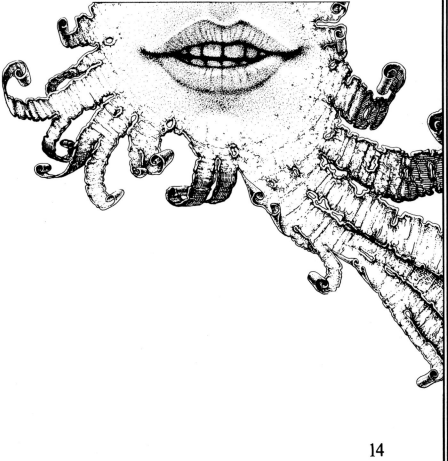

Above: THE HEADSCRATCHER. Ink line and wash.
The function of art can often be to exorcise the demon.

Here is one of my worst nightmares: yet when I had nailed the demon to the paper, it died.

Section Two:
THE EVOLUTION OF A PERSONAL STYLE

A period of upheaval followed, in which I had to teach full-time to support our new family. A cramped and hectic environment did not help my work.

Many new projects began and foundered — children's books, fantasies for adults, new ideas for three-dimensional and even moving paintings.

I made several trips to London to try to get work as an illustrator, but was repeatedly told that I should write my own books to fit my own pictures, as my style was so specific. *Daniel Buttonweed and the Siege of Granite Rock* was a rambling and moralising adventure story, complete with maps and several sample illustrations. But no publisher was interested, and I began to make rather a bitter collection of rejection slips. The tide turned when we bought a house of our own: suddenly I had both space and privacy. I converted the children's book into a shorter story for younger children, and under the new title *Micky's New Home*, it met with a much more favourable response.

It was also at about this time that Peter and Kathryn Jones came on the scene. Peter Jones was at that time Assistant Director of the Welsh Arts Council, and his enthusiasm for my work was a great encouragement to me. He would visit about once a year, and each time I would make sure that I had plenty of new work to show him.

HUNTING PARTY AT THE WORLD'S END. Oil on panel. Diameter 510 mm. 1967. (Reproduced by permission of John Enders).

In his children's book *The Voyage of the Dawntreader,* C. S. Lewis describes a land far away at the edge of the world. At first this painting was intended to show a view from a porthole of the ship, but gradually the irrelevancies multiplied so much that I decided that it represented a hunting party led by some mythical king.

The air is dense like water, and the weightlessness allows the participants in this slow yet joyful drama to float about like dancers in an aerial ballet.

THE SUMMERHOUSE. Oil on panel. Diameter 460 mm.
1972. (Reproduced by permission of Mrs. Brennand).

Five years separate this painting from the one on the
previous page, but I have put then together because they both
try to express the same feelings. Here, again in an almost
weightless environment, I have made a playground for my
two children, Danny and Rosie, where all the animals are
friends, and where the sun always shines down on a world
buzzing with activity.

There are some primitive rocket-ships here too—
whimsical fore-runners of the space-craft I have drawn more
recently to illustrate the covers of science-fiction books.
Creatures come into being from the very soil like plants ger-
minating. The tortoise is born under a cherry tree and
surprises the gardener when it gets up and walks like a hermit
crab with a sea-anemone growing on its shell.

19

Illustrations for DANIEL BUTTONWEED & THE SIEGE
OF GRANITE ROCK. Ink line and wash.
An anti-war story for children.
Top left: 'Skipper returns to Knar'
Top right: 'Daniel in the Cage'
Lower left: 'The Troops of Granite Rock'
Lower right: 'The Guns of Redbeard'

Above: INVASION FROM MARS! Ink.

This drawing was a reaction to the sort of S-F which can only envisage malevolent invasions from space. My Martians are on a picnic. Later on, commissions dictated that I should perpetuate the myth of the wicked extra-terrestrial.

Next Page: HIS MAJESTY'S SHIP GOLDEN LEAVES FOR THE WORLD'S END. Watercolour and gold leaf. 690 mm x 460 mm. (Reproduced by permission of Jenkins Lowery).

A ceremonial event in a fairyland kingdom. The beginning of a quest. The mythology is drawn from a sort of 'Genesis' chapter in a fantasy for adults which I began in 1968 but is still unfinished.

GOLDEN SYRU

GOLDEN

Above: OILY DOLL FOUND ON THE SEASHORE. Pencil: actual size.
What ravishment has soiled your rose flesh?
The sea would take you: yet you took the sea by storm.
Lovely legless torso, daughter of the rainbow.

Opposite: SALLY, THE DOLL WITH THE BROKEN EYE. Pencil: actual size.
    Dolls always seem more beautiful when they have aged; they get a patina from fond children's fingers. And the pathos is heightened when they have received some injury, for the illusion of life is still greater.

Pages 26-27: MASKED BALL. Watercolour. (Reproduced by permission of Kathryn Shelton-Jones).
    "The gods have come to Earth to visit: Zeus appears as a swan to Leda. The teal, monarch of the lake, bears his willing passenger to some hidden place where they may exchange caresses. The colibris in mystic joy solemnise the glory of their progeny, safely stored in the tortoise's carapace. The knight, finely clothed for mock aggression, bears off the mannikin's child, who flees coquettish from his boyish advances. Here the serpent hugs the limbs of his companion: festivities await them beyond imagining. The ancient scholar, newly freed from his dark library, finds joy within unexpected embraces. "I'm a tiger!" says the girl with the platinum hair. Her borrowed pelt invites caresses. The Rainbow Man, meteorodynamic, spirit of the storm, spins in at the double doors. This is a masked ball. Watch out! It's just beginning!"

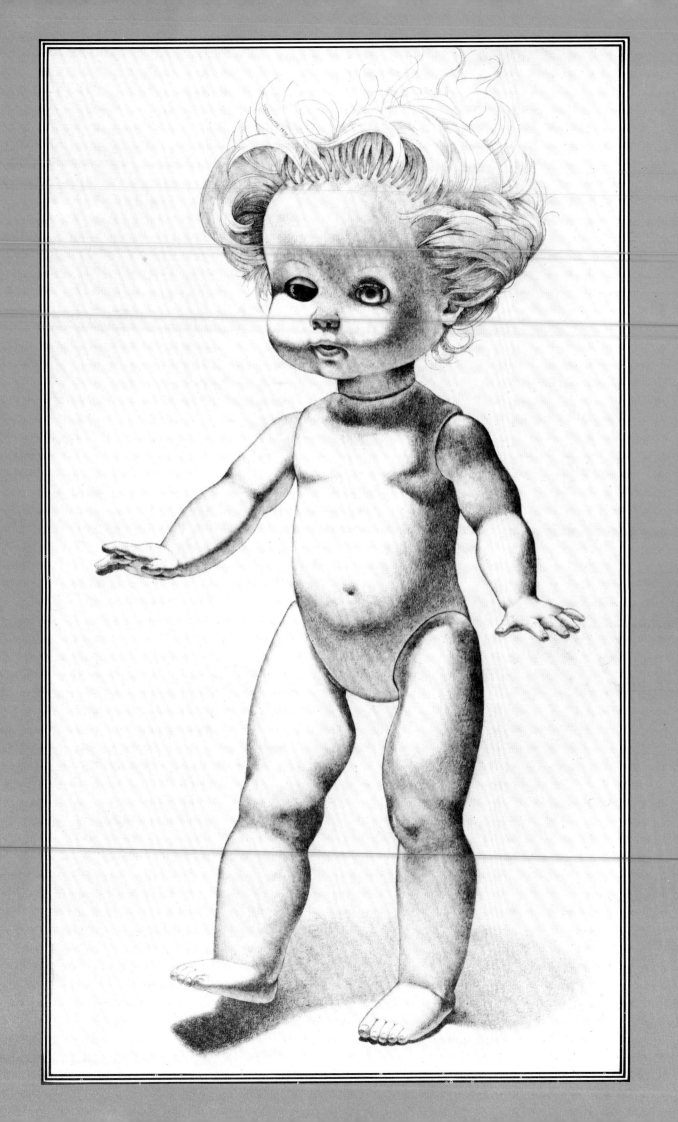

The illustrations on these two pages are from a series of small collages in which I experimented with the traditional collage device of surprise. The images are merely cuttings from magazines combined to give a compelling, even horrific, new twist to photographic material. The ambiguity of scale, the unlikely juxtaposition of familiar objects, fascinated me. It is because I like visual surprises that I have enjoyed illustrating science-fiction book covers.

One of the most important influences on my work has been the poetry of Edith Sitwell, particularly as it appears in Walton's *Façade*. The words are almost nonsense, but they conjure up an atmosphere of delightful girlish naughtiness and irreverence—a direct reaction to the stern humourlessness of Victorian England and Empire.

Her poems have given me an inexhaustible source of images. Her characters, like Daisy and Lily, Rose and Alice, have entered my own personal mythology, along with figures from my own writing and from the Christian religion.

Left: EPIPHANY. Watercolour and gold leaf.
    The three wise men visit the infant and the virgin mother.

Above: MARINER MAN. Watercolour. (In the collection of Christine Restall).
    A poem from Edith Sitwell's *Façade*. "What are you staring at, mariner man..?"

Below left: WE BEAR VELVET CREAM (detail). Watercolour.
    Another Sitwell poem.
    "We bear velvet cream, green and babyish;
    Small leaves seem, each stream
    Horses' tails that swish..."
    A vision of alpine bliss, milky soft and invitingly female.

Below right: GREENWEED AND HORNBEAM. Watercolour. (In the collection of Gordon Rattray-Taylor).
    Two characters from *Daniel Buttonweed*.

UNTO US A SON IS GIVEN. Oil on panel.

Heavily influenced by the work of early Flemish painters, the composition of this madonna and child is based on the eastern symbol of life—the Tai-gi-tu—which appears to rotate in both directions or to break like a wave.

The sweet and sour colours of the fruit in the foreground symbolise the joys and tragedies that await the new arrival on Earth. The anatomy is deliberately wrong for I felt I should distort the figure in such a way as to express love and warmth. I began this painting when Danny was born,

but altered and added to it over several years, scraping away areas of paint so that I could work directly on the white ground.

Up to now most of my oil paintings had been done in just one coat of paint, but here I began to see that, as in decorating, two coats are often better than one. The bright green of the mantle was obtained by a thin glaze of green applied over an underpainting of yellow. The title comes from Handel's "Messiah."

31

Above: MICKY IN HIS CAVE. Etching and drypoint.

Section Three:
ETCHING AND ENGRAVING (INTAGLIO PRINTING)

The term 'intaglio' covers all processes of printing in which the image is etched, cut or scratched on a metal plate. The ink is trapped in the lines below the surface of the plate and is transferred to the paper by rolling both plate and paper through a press. The fact that the paper is pushed into the lines gives intaglio its character — that is, that the printed image stands out above the rest of the paper. Banknotes and visiting cards are often printed in this way.

The most widely practised type of intaglio today is etching — of all the media available to the artist, etching must be one of the most exciting, exasperating, unpredictable, yet potentially one of the most rewarding and subtle.

This is what the process involves. A polished plate of copper, zinc or steel, is first coated very thinly with a specially prepared acid-resistant wax or 'ground'. The plate must be absolutely clean, or the ground may come off during the rest of the process. The grounded plate is then smoked with tapers to darken and harden it. The plate is then 'needled': that is, the ground is removed with a needle or some similar tool, revealing the shining copper underneath. The plate is then exposed to acid in a bath, so that the metal is eaten away, but only where the ground has been scratched off. The remaining ground is later cleaned off, and the plate is ready for printing.

When the plate is being needled, the shining lines made on the plate will eventually print black on white. The image will also be reversed as in a mirror. So the artist is really working in the dark — on the reversed negative! But this uncertainty is what makes the process so exciting: you never know quite how a print is going to turn out. When printing, the plate is first heated, so that the rather glutinous ink can melt over it and be dabbed and pushed firmly into all the etched lines. Next the surface of the plate must be wiped clean in such a way as to leave ink in the etched lines. This is usually done first with coarsely woven scrim, then with the palm of the hand. The printing paper is soaked in water and partially dried so that it is soft but not wet. This is usually done on the preceding day. Paper and plate are then passed through the press, and the image is transferred

33

Above: POLKA. Drypoint engraving and etching tinted with watercolours and inks.

This was a second attempt at Robinson Crusoe's wish-fulfilling dream, as mentioned in Edith Sitwell's poem of the same name. I began work on this plate in drypoint only, for at that time I had no proper facilities for etching with acids. I also had no press and the proofs of the first state were pulled on an old mangle.

Above: THE EVOLUTION OF A PLATE.

The history of a plate could go on indefinitely, for modifications and additions can be made at will. These separate prints are called 'states'. An 'edition' (a limited number of signed prints) is usually pulled from the final state.

from one to the other. It is difficult to describe the moment when the paper is first peeled off the plate. You can see the print reflected in the shining surface of the plate—but is it too dark or too light? Did the drawing look better in reverse? After days or even weeks of careful work on the plate, the whole thing could be a failure.

Below left: MYSTIC ROSEMARY. Etching from three plates.

The 'mystic rose' is a very beautiful and amazing mathematical phenomenon. I had made several large drawings of it before working on this plate—one as an ellipse, and one in perspective, which was quite an exercise in patience.

My daughter Rosemary is also a mystic phenomenon! So I put them together to make a pun. In fact the drawing was done from one of Rosie's dolls—it was better than she was at keeping still. The marbled effect was obtained by flicking stop-out varnish between successive 'open bites'.

Below right: MOTHER AND CHILD. Etching and aquatint.

A rather unsatisfactory attempt to reproduce part of the painting *Unto Us a Son is Given* (see page 31). The gradations in tone were obtained by spraying diluted stop-out onto an aquatint ground by means of an air-brush. The second colour was rolled onto the surface of the plate.

Above: EXPÉRIENCES TORTOLOGIQUES. Etching: actual size.

Themes from the oil painting *The Summerhouse* reproduced on page 19. Some more creatures from my bestiary. This plate was removed from the acid several times, so that areas where I wanted thinner, paler lines could be 'stopped out' to prevent them deepening and widening.

But the joy when things go right amply compensates for all the disasters, and there are few errors that cannot be at least partially corrected. Any lines or tones etched into the plate —provided they are not too deep—may be removed by simply scraping away the metal. However, it is rather difficult to do this without leaving tiny ink-retaining scratches, which will of course show up on the print. Other methods of making a plate include:

DRYPOINT ENGRAVING: Here the image is scratched on an ungrounded plate with a needle. No acid is needed. Plastic sheet may be used instead of metal.

BURIN ENGRAVING: Again working on an ungrounded plate, the image is cut with a tool rather like a small chisel.

AQUATINT: Powdered resin is sprinkled over the plate and melted, thus making a ground full of tiny holes. When etched, areas of flat tone are made. Parts not to be etched are 'stopped out' with varnish. Gradations in tone may be obtained by spraying on the stop-out varnish with an air-brush.

SOFT GROUND ETCHING: A sticky ground can be applied to the plate so that when textured materials are pressed into it, the ground is removed, leaving an impression of the weave or texture. This method is excellent for reproducing lace and other patterns. (See *Réveil* on page 47).

Above: WHO'S BEEN EATING MY MUSHROOMS?
Etching: actual size.

Danny's toy rabbit encounters the real thing!

The time spent in the acid bath is critical. It could take anything from five minutes to five hours to get the required strength of line. Unfortunately the distant areas of this print are slightly over-bitten.

On page 39: FORTINBRASSO. Etching, drypoint and aquatint.

Another homage to tin cans. The knight also owes much of his character to Tenniel, Heath-Robinson and even Cervantes. The verse, however, is my own.

"When morning had polished her brazen dish
Fortinbrasso would ride on a golden fish
Fortinbrasso would seek some innocent fun
And go to tilt with the golden sun."

The gradations in tone were achieved by spraying stop-out varnish with an air-brush.

On page 39: SYMBIOSIS. Etching from eight plates.

The symbiotic snails have a common dwelling but no common purpose. Fear makes the whistling puffer fish breathe in and swell, but when it breathes out the whistle will blow. The serpent creeps from the paint tube. Propagandist power creeps from the image.

Above: MUSHROOM FARM. Etching and drypoint, tinted with watercolour and ink.

The making of the plate was in two stages: first the etching; secondly, the drypoint, of which the fragile 'burr' only just survived long enough to produce an edition of fifty.

Unable to find a publisher for *Micky's New Home*, I considered printing all the illustrations myself as etchings, tinting them, and binding them as a book. But I had not considered how much work it would involve, and more important, how much such a book would have to cost! Having sold the first edition of tinted prints, I later tinted further small editions, using different colour schemes. The total number of prints however, as in all my editions, remained limited to fifty.

FORTINBRASSO. (See page 37).

Right: THE MARIONETTE. Drypoint and etching from two plates.

One of many etchings I produced while working on the triptych *The Thousand-Year Roundabout.* (See Section 4 page 49).

SYMBIOSIS. (See page 37).

Left: SALLY, THE DOLL WITH THE BROKEN EYE. Etching. (Also produced as a colour print using a second plate).

This was a rather inadequate attempt to multiply the pencil drawing reproduced on page 25. I added a line or two from another Sitwell poem: 'Rose and Alice'.

Below left: METEORODYNAMIC GUN. Etching.

Contemporary with the triptych *The Thousand-Year Roundabout* (see Section 4). One of a series of etchings showing themes from the painting.

The meteorodynamic gun has its origins in the earlier painting *Masked Ball* (see pages 26 and 27), but here it has become a symbol of aggression rather than of the benign dynamism of the elements.

Below right: THE SIEGE ENGINE. Etching. (See the triptych in Section 4).

As a beginner, I would bite the plate only once, and all lines had an equal thickness and strength. This plate should have been removed from the acid from time to time to stop-out areas which ought to have been lighter and more delicate.

"Micky & Friend" Patrick Woodroffe, July 1973.

9/50

Above: MICKY AND FRIEND. Etching: actual size.

Another etching based on an illustration for *Micky's New Home*, this plate was repeatedly stopped-out during biting so as to make a variety of line thicknesses.

Right: A LITTLE BESTIARY. Etching with soft and hard grounds.

A catalogue of some of the beasts from my personal mythology.

"Drawings made carefully in the wild from living specimens.

"THE OPIUM VAT—meteorodynamic, a receptacle for the distillations of soil, rain and sunshine. He is the sand-scatterer. His sleepy message is addressed to all. All must drink from the opium vat.

"THE HERMIT ELEPHANT—the huge becomes tiny—these snail-elephants are in a flux of emergence. They are the true gasteropods. Their tusks—antennae for feeling the way—are pliable yet firm. Their trunks are the complement of their shells. They are an emergent species endowed with vast good sense and humour. They have not yet shown what they are capable of.

"THE LION—we find by the rain-soaked kerb, a humble pilgrim. His tiny talons are velveted and he has all but unlearned his snarling."

41

Above: DAISY AND LILY. Etching and drypoint tinted with watercolour and ink.

Another piece of Edith Sitwell's mythology; Daisy and Lily (lazy and silly) admire their own splendid finery as they strut along a fashionable beach. Edith Sitwell does not specify that they are a falcon and a lamb—that's just the way I see them.

It was while I was working on this idea that I was commissioned to do the cover paintings for a series of books by Dashiell Hammett. Obsessed by Daisy and Lily, I saw the first book *The Maltese Falcon* as a sort of dream-chasing adventure, and used the same figure on my first design for the cover. Unfortunately, but perhaps not surprisingly, the publishers did not consider the idea appropriate, and I was asked to produce another painting—this time representing an ordinary falcon. In the end neither ideas were used, and to make things worse, the second painting went missing in America.

42

"ALICE" Patrick Woodroffe 1973   33/50

Above: ALICE. Etching from three plates.

Oh, what visions are conjured up by girls' names!

The problem of registration (that is, to position all plates exactly) is always hard in colour printmaking, especially as the paper is likely to stretch during the printing process owing to the pressure of the press. For small plates it can work very well, but the larger the plate the greater the likelihood of poor registration. This plate, which measures 300 x 250mm, is just about at the limit for colour etching.

Two of the plates have ink in the etched lines (intaglio), while the third has colour rolled onto the surface, leaving the intaglio white.

Above: MICKY'S NEW HOME. (See page 48).

Opposite: ALPHABET FOR MICKY. (See page 48).

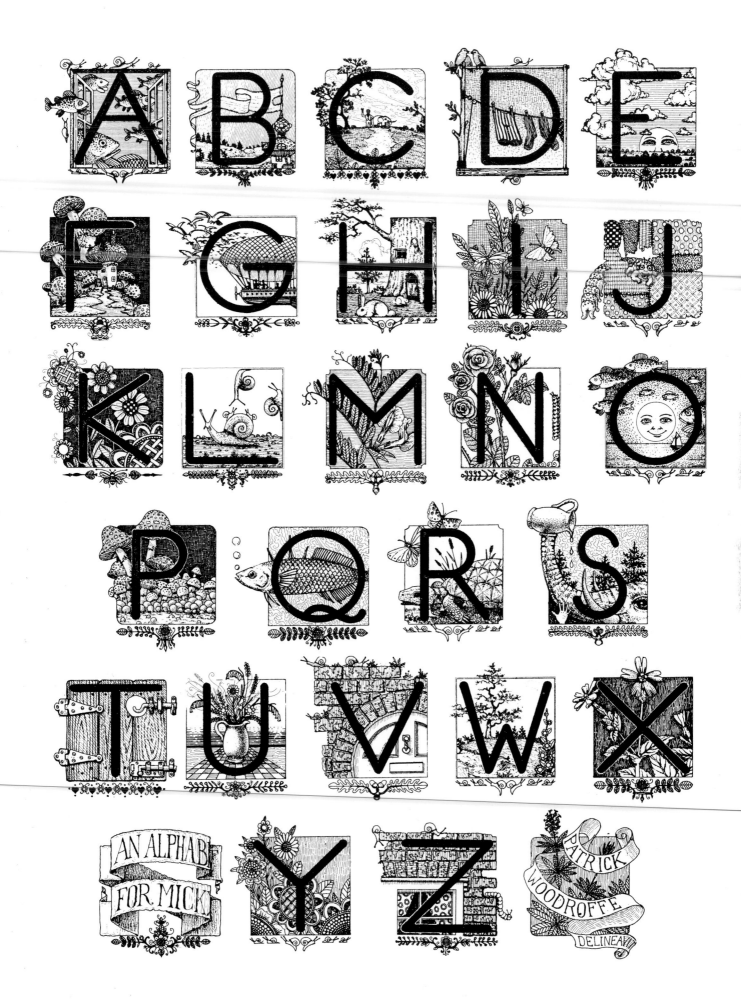

AN ALPHABET FOR MICK

PATRICK WOODROFFE DELINEAVIT

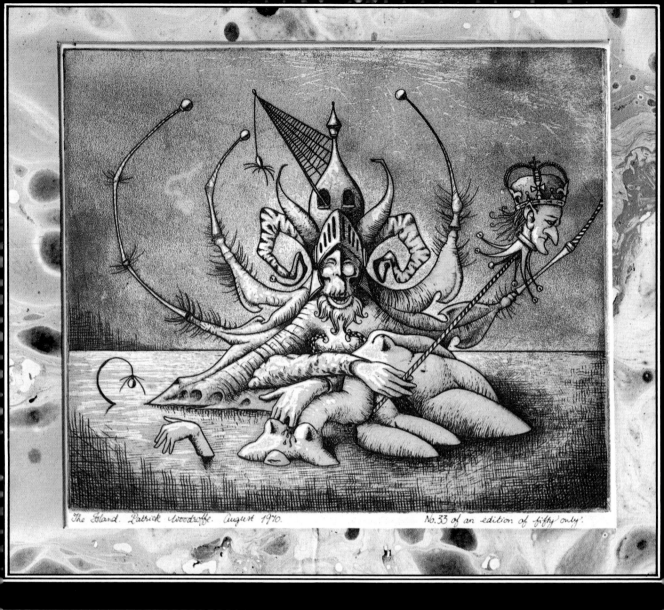

The Island. Patrick Woodroffe. August 1970.   No. 33 of an edition of fifty only.

Above: THE LAST MOONSHOT. (See page 48).

Opposite page, top: THE ISLAND. (See page 48).

Opposite page, lower left: ASTROSAURUS. (See page 48).

Opposite page, lower right: THE SCULPTOR AND HIS MODEL. (See page 48).

Above: BABY DRYAD. A drypoint engraving later etched over.

Below: ELLE A TORT, LA TORTUE? Etching from three plates.

    The inspiration was the completion of the Concorde and its feared effects on the atmosphere.

    ("Is the tortoise wrong?" asks the title.)

Below: RÉVEIL. Etching from two plates.

    When one of this pair of symbiotic tortoises is asleep, the other may take it where it chooses.

Above: ROYAL BAKING POWDER. Etching and aquatint.
    Another print showing the influence of Heath-Robinson.

On page 44: MICKY'S NEW HOME. Etching and aquatint.
    Another idea for the children's book of the same name. This print involved the use of a process known as 'open bite', in which the entire foreground was stopped-out, and the acid was allowed to eat away the plate over the sky area; the two levels of plate thus obtained give a soft edge of ink around the house and plants. The aquatint was applied after that, and the plate was bitten partly in and partly out of the acid bath, so that a gradation of tone was possible. This effect is known as 'creeping bite'.

On page 45: ALPHABET FOR MICKY. Etching.
    An alphabet of initials for the text of *Micky's New Home*.

On page 46: THE ISLAND.
    A drypoint later etched over. I added a second plate too. This one was a surface print: the ink was rolled onto the surface of the plate, thus leaving the intaglio free of ink. The next plate was printed on top of this without removing the paper from the press.

On page 46: ASTROSAURUS.
    A much more recent etching, dashed off between urgent commissioned work. Heath-Robinson inspired bumblings are light relief after hard-selling book-jacket designs.

On page 46: THE SCULPTOR AND HIS MODEL.
    My first ever etching. The whole thing was completed in a single evening. It was 'bitten' (exposed to the acid) in the kitchen sink.

On page 47: THE LAST MOONSHOT. Etching from four plates.
    To celebrate the last US Moon landing, my last 'Keep Smiling' face? Here I used a process called 'sand grain'. The grounded plate is run through the press several times with a piece of sandpaper to make a tone rather like aquatint.

Section Four:
TRIPTYCH: THE THOUSAND-YEAR ROUNDABOUT.
Oil panels: 675 x 295   675 x 675   675 x 295

One of the advantages of painting over literature is that you can say all kinds of things at the same time, and that each separate statement can be taken different ways. A painting as complex as this can have no definitive interpretation — not even I who painted it can be aware of all the subconscious symbolism that creeps in without my knowledge.

The triptych is an act of exploration, a kind of visual hypothesis. Looking forward to the end of this century — to the end of the second millennium — it reviews the history of man and his mythologies. In common with the series of drawings *The Child-Stealers*, it has as its central character an innocent child faced with the hostility and deception of the outside world.

The picture evolved over a period of several years, and the ideas evolved as it was painted. It did not spring into my mind as a complete vision, indeed it began as an epiphany, complete with Mary and Joseph, shepherds and wise men! So

the child was originally intended to represent Christ, but now he represents all men.

And the saplings already grow from which our crosses will be made. Millennia have followed, tumbling over each other in their haste. And soon the millennium shall come when all the strivings of the past shall be fulfilled. These last few years have mud on their boots; their haste is greater, but these last few hours tick away far more slowly than the first. The millennia are a carousel, a thousand-year roundabout. Soon the carousel will jar to a sudden halt, and we must all climb off, the pleasures of childhood gone, along with its fears and follies. At last we shall stand, mature yet with fresh minds, on the threshold of our inheritance, and make our first steps outwards in search of the gods we once knew so well.

Man is a passenger on an old planet. His ride is a long trek from the middle of time to the end of time. Those who took the roads were young and old, babes and crones, guided by princes, potentates, presidents — the key-holders of temporal power, whose purple skirts, digitalis-like, brought venomous oblivion. They trod the upward and the downward pathways, unwilling, sobbing, rattling with fear.

On the hillside burgeoned a red tree, and though the evil in its fruits was a myth, none dared pluck them nor consume the windfalls. The snake-tree of Lerna was a self-devouring yet a self-regenerating thing, a symbol both of hope and despair, both of life and of death.

On page 50: Upper left volet: THE PATHWAY TO THE SKY.

The Earth is the flesh of Daedalus, the death-escaper; his bones are as air, a flying spectrum flung up from the pit. He only has the poppies of sleep to help him forget the horror of immortality. Such is true transfiguration, for springing from his hands that moulder in the soil, no sooner has he drawn his last breath, come shining nymphs, infant dryads.

The pit was a shattered city, yet more populous by far than in the days of its splendour. And the windows of hell were papered over with pseudo-landscapes that gave empty reassurance to the condemned. Counterfeit love, half hidden in the murk, thrust lethargically to the rhythms of a depraved lust.

Beyond the hill the sea slips away into the chasms of the earth, while the fleets of men squabble over the possession of it. The lion and the cockerel are well matched, and their battle will never end.

It was surely a mistake to personify good and evil as the ancients did. It was a neat idea which enabled metaphysics to be accommodated in literature—but it led to an impasse. The gods come down to manifest themselves to a pre-occupied world; in such a dualism, who could believe in the allmight of a humble god? The angels in the clouds covered their eyes when they saw how men ignored the puppetry of Emmanuel rising on the third day.

52

Above: Lower left quarter of central panel: ASSAULT ON THE FORTRESS.

The child lies secure for a time in the cathedral-fortress—in the enceinte—watched over by the mystic symbols of humility and love, caressed by soft lawns and the scents of garden flowers. A garden is an asylum; all the conflicts of the species are decided at a stroke, and the gardener's trowel is quick.

Yet outside the fortress there is no gardener: he has drifted off among the stars, and disputes must settle themselves. Even the elements must fight for survival.

Men said that humility was a virtue, yet the lion, were he to clothe himself in humility, would be nothing more than an emblem; he could not defend your gates. All around, the hermit ele-phants die, giving their lives seemingly in vain, for ranged against them come the multitudes of follies, masks, disguises, fantasies, lies, fictions—creeping from the depths of the human past, the black night-memories that haunt us all. Even masks disguise themselves and make our senses reel.

Three seek direct attack on the fortress. Others wait for maturity, when the babe shall walk out and be seduced.

First the trebuchet, taking female form, clothes itself in the cadaver of a broken doll, and seeks suitable range. The doll weeps for the misuse of her spoiled body. Next comes the thundering phallus of the meteorodynamic gun, half joyful, half agonised, potent beyond measure, twin faces grimace in a paroxysm of ejaculation,

DROFFT 1972

Opposite: Upper right central panel: THE EPICENTRE.

Above: Lower right central panel: THE SPATIAL AND TEMPORAL RIFT.

the ivresse of absolute power. Then the opium vat, indolent, lethargic, selling apathy and oblivion. Biafra slices itself neatly at the waist with an axe.

At the top of the rise, its finger-roots groping in the soil, is a tree whose fanged leaves may trap unwary travellers, dupe them, induce them to serve it as a totem. This is the vanity and stupidity of art. Close by is the sculptor, who, mistaking his model for the stone, destroys her with his chisel. He is the man who sets art in place of reality and worships it.

A single point in time and space pours forth the whole universe—yet it also engulfs it. Indeed the universe is daily both created and devoured.

That single point is the eternal departure point, the only destination of matter. All trains travel both to it and from it, no matter where they go.

The fool runs along the burning beach; he has seen the scurrying clouds, felt the hot stones under his feet. If he were a wise man he would bathe in the sea and let himself be swallowed up.

How can we accept the meagre metaphysics of the past, when we know what we know now? Beyond the battling mountains, beyond the writing in the sky, are other dimensions undreamed of by our ancestors. Other worlds where sweet red winds blow, and where maidens sit forever young and velvet-creamy in flower fragrant meadows.

Opposite: Upper right volet.   Above: Lower right volet: A SECOND NOAH'S ARK.

Beneath the superficial appearance of space are other dimensions, ambiguities of perspective. Here new worlds are born and die. The fool was frightened by the constant flux of matter, but it need not frighten *us*. It is the fluidity that gives the dynamism. Without beginnings and endings—however illusory—there can be no illusion of change.

The blueprints come to life. The moths that have lain so long in pupae, emerge in splendour. This is a new resurrection—Daedalus lives! The spires of the new religion are the gleaming edifices of space technology. We shall be a new race—a race with winged feet.

How can the mythologies of the past count for much for us? We must make our own.

The triptych was completed in 1972.

THE THORN APPLE TREE
"you don't expect thorns on an apple tree"
WOODROFFE JAN. 1971

Above: THE THORN APPLE TREE.

Dolls in distress again. As in earlier drawings, I found here that to use dolls as models is a good way to express pathos. Here I have tried to show the anxiety of parenthood, the anxiety we feel when we see imminent calamities that the child does not suspect.

Section Five:
"THE CHILD-STEALERS"

The three drawings on the following pages were a direct reaction to fatherhood. The responsibilities are sufficient to give one pause, but for me it was the fact that my flesh had somehow divided that made me think.

MADAME PERSEPHONE ON HOLIDAY BY THE SEASIDE

She was the stealer of warm sheets,
She sat on the hill at the day's end;
And taking the sun for a warming-pan,
She knitted a mantle of Plantain.

She was the stealer of good dreams,
She sat on a moon at the world's end,
And taking the Earth for a ball of thread,
She fitted some curtains
And went to bed.

PATRICK WOODROFFE JANUARY NINETEEN SEVENTY-ONE

Opposite: MADAME PERSEPHONE ON HOLIDAY BY THE SEA.

Just as the parent cannot protect the child from the world outside, he is even less capable of shielding her from the world inside her own head. Her nightmare is an intimation of mortality and the fragility of her security.

The verse reads:

She was the stealer of warm sheets,
She sat on the sill at the day's end:
And taking the sun for a warming-pan,
Knitted a mantle of tarlatan.

She was the stealer of good dreams,
She sat on a stool at the world's end:
And taking the Earth for a ball of thread,
Fitted some curtains
And went to bed.

Above: TEREUS GOES BIRDNESTING.

Here is the final stage of the life-cycle of the emergent moth—the emergent woman. In the language of the entomologist, 'larva' means 'mask' and 'pupa' means 'doll'. Will the emergent moth, its wings scarcely unfolded from the chrysalis, be at once consumed by a predator?

The Tereus of Greek mythology violated his sister-in-law Philomela, and cut out her tongue so that she could not tell. However, Philomela made an embroidery which told the story, and all protagonists were turned into birds, Tereus into a hoopoe and Philomela into a nightingale.

I am often asked why I did not finish *Tereus*. For once I felt that it had all been said, and that I could abandon it here.

The pale figures are drawn in silverpoint, that is, a piece of silver has been used instead of a pencil. The paper must first be given a coat of hard paint so that the silver will take, and not simply scratch away the paper.

The verse reads:

He was the spoiler of birds' nests
He plundered the eggs from the warm womb
And taking them off to a quiet spot
Boiled them four minutes and ate the lot.

He was the freezer of soft flesh
He severed the tongues of ravished girls.
Yet broderie spoke
When the voice-box broke
And needle-like long
The nightingale's song told all.

61

Above: I'M COMING TO GET YOU! Oil on wood.

One of my earliest attempts to achieve a three-dimensional image. It is intended to represent the one-way flow of energy from the Sun to the Earth.

The picture was made to be accommodated in an existing frame. The pegs are made from dowelling, as at that time I had no lathe.

Section Six:
THREE-DIMENSIONAL PROJECTS

Film animation, had I been able to afford it, would have attracted me as the logical next step in making the image more real, but it is not the only way. One can use three dimensions instead of two; the objects shown here are neither paintings nor sculptures—they are both.

The pegs or skittles were in most cases cut on a lathe, and the stripes were painted in emulsions, enamels and fluorescent paints by rotating the pegs very slowly on the lathe bed.

Above left: SPECIMEN CABINET. Oil on wood, glass.

In this painting I have used glass rod, drawn over a flame and set into holes in the wood. The butterflies and moths are only partially authentic.

As with most of my three-dimensional projects, this picture is heavy and cumbersome, hard to keep clean and difficult to transport. Since that time I have tried to make this sort of object much smaller.

Above right: COSMIC PARADOX. Oil on wood, copper sheet.

Perhaps the curvature of space is such that, as in a distorting mirror, we look at our own reflections but imagine we see strangers.

The little round faces obsess me still, though I have painted hundreds of them. I have tried to trace their origins, and have come to the conclusion that they came from the old 'Guinness' adverts — the smiling moon face in the foam, which looked so much like my father. Perhaps they also owe a great deal to a grandfather clock we used to have when I was a child: I can remember admiring the beautiful way its Sun and Moon were painted on a revolving dial. It is their simplicity that appeals to me; they are a sort of code-word, a heiroglyphic for joy.

Left: FANFARE FOR THE SUN. Oil on wood, copper sheet.

A much more recent treatment of the Sun-worshipping theme of *I'm Coming to Get You!* (See previous page). The wooden skittles were both cut and painted on a lathe, and are set in a copper sheet intended to reflect them in such a way that they appear to be coming into the room through a hole in the wall.

64

Right: UNFINISHED ARTICULATED DOLL.

She was made for a 'painting' which was to be not only three-dimensional, but also mobile. The doll was to be so arranged that she could be made to move by pulling wires attached to her limbs through the back of the picture. The project also involved a baby doll and several other elements.

But the weight—the doll's head is carved from solid mahogany—became a crucial factor, and the sheer physical limitations of the materials brought the project to an unsatisfactory end. The hair is human, from my wife Jean.

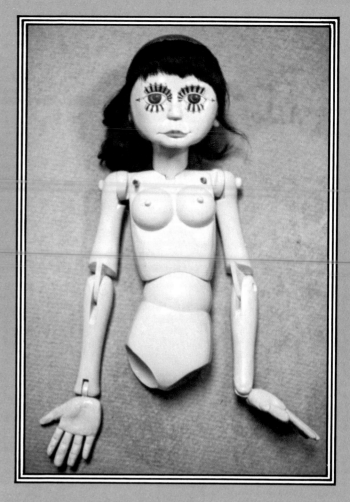

Below left: PLEIAD. Oil on wood.

Seven stars for the seven days. The wooden pegs can be rotated from below to reveal or hide the faces.

Below right: THE EVERLASTING COVENANT. Oil on wood.

Genesis IX 16:

"And the bow shall be in the cloud, and I will look upon it, that I may remember the everlasting covenant between God and every living creature of all flesh that is upon the Earth."

I carved the window in which these faces are set from part of an old bank counter given to me by a friend.

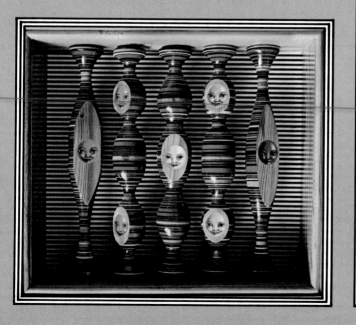

Above: BIRD BOX. Oil on wood, tin cans, snail-shells, wire, glass etc.

This modest palace for our feathered friends spent several futile years in our garden before its transformation. No birds would nest there, though the snails appreciated it in the winter. So I brought it inside and decorated it—leaving other boxes for the snails to hibernate in. It is filled with empty snail-shells glued to the walls.

There is a connection here with another of Edith Sitwell's poems:

"Lovely bird, will you stay and sing,
Flirting your sheenèd wing
Peck with your beak and cling
To our balconies?"

Above: Cover Art for *The Sailor on the Seas of Fate* by
Michael Moorcock, published by Quartet Books Ltd., London.

Sections Seven to Thirteen:
BOOK JACKETS

In 1972 I felt I had to retire from teaching. Evan Anthony, at that time art critic for *The Spectator,* offered me an exhibition at his Covent Garden Gallery. The show was a great success, and was twice extended. I sold quite a number of paintings and drawings and several hundred etchings.

But then—more important for me at that time, when I had to ensure a regular income—David Larkin, art director for Pan Books, offered me my first commission for a book jacket *(Day*

Above: Some of the 'proofs' of my book jacket paintings.
These are the samples which the printer sends to the
art director for approval before going into production.

Million see page 124). From then on I was rarely short of work. Indeed over the next three years the whole thing grew to such an extent that I found myself booked up several months in advance, working not only for most paperback publishers in the U.K., but also, through an agency (Michael Brodie's 'Artists International') for the U.S.A.

Normally the job involved reading the book first, which has made me change many of my opinions about science-fiction. For one thing it has improved my taste, but it has also dulled my appetite for other people's fantasies! After submission and approval of a 'rough' (sketch), the final artwork took me, on average, about a week,

so that during the next three years I produced about ninety paintings for book jackets. I still find it thrilling to see my work printed: it must surely be the ambition of most painters to reach as wide a public as possible.

In 1975 the cartoonist Mel Calman offered me a show at his gallery 'The Workshop' in Lamb's Conduit Street, London. This was an exhibition of original artwork for book jackets and record sleeves, together with a selection of etchings. It was there that I met 'Dragon's Dream', and Hubert Schaafsma and Roger Dean offered me the opportunity of producing this book.

Above: Cover Art for *The Sleeping Sorceress* by Michael
Moorcock, published by Quartet Books Ltd., London.
Acrylic gouache, crayon and ink.

Section Seven:
MICHAEL MOORCOCK

Mike Jarvis, art director for Quartet Books,
eventually commissioned from me paintings for
almost all the Moorcock books on their list.
Moorcock's prolific and vividly imaginative work,
ranging as it does over many worlds and many
times, has proved to be in tune with the present-
day need for escapist literature. In his books
nothing is impossible, nothing unacceptable. His
monsters, machines and improbable worlds do
not need to be feasible: he is not writing for
devotees of Arthur C. Clarke, but for all those
bereaved disciples of J. R. R. Tolkien who are
seeking someone fit to wear the master's mantle.

Above: Cover Art for *The Bull and the Spear* by Michael Moorcock, published by Quartet Books Ltd., London. Acrylic gouache, crayon and ink.

This was the first volume of *The Chronicle of Prince Corum and the Silver Hand*. In order to indicate the variety and mystery of the contents—a book jacket is, after all, nothing more than a form of packaging—I combined various elements from the story in a 'composite' which owes much to the sixteenth-century Milanese painter Guiseppe Arcimboldo, whose strange fruit and vegetable compositions made allegedly recognisable portraits. I was now committed to this type of composition for the other books in the series.

Above: Cover Art for *The Oak and the Ram* by Michael Moorcock, published by Quartet Books Ltd., London. Acrylic gouache, crayon and ink. (Original artwork in the collection of Anthony Fry).

To illustrate the second volume of *The Chronicle of Prince Corum and the Silver Hand,* I tried to show the strange mixture of savagery and mysticism which pervades Moorcock's work.

Above: Cover Art for *The English Assassin* by Michael Moorcock, published by Quartet Books Ltd., London. Acrylic gouache, crayon and ink. (Reproduced by permission of Brinley Morris).

This is one of Michael Moorcock's Jerry Cornelius novels, in which the hero appears in various guises and various sexes, but mainly as the Carnaby Street dandy. Periodically Cornelius must undergo a process of marine rejuvenation.

Above: Cover Art for *A Cure for Cancer* by Michael Moorcock, published by Quartet Books Ltd., London. Acrylic gouache, crayon and ink.

Another Jerry Cornelius book, of which the main ingredients are violence and ambiguous sexuality.

Above: Cover Art for *The Sword and the Stallion* by Michael Moorcock, published by Quartet Books Ltd., London. Acrylic gouache, crayon, ink and marbling.

The third volume of *The Chronicle of Prince Corum and the Silver Hand*, this is a lugubrious and mystical tale of daring deeds in a mythical world of dwarves, dragons and wizards.

It is one of the many covers on which I have used a 'marbled' background, though in this case the random marbling was manipulated so as to be integrated into the sky and landscape. Oil-based colour floating on water is picked up by placing the painting face downwards on the surface. Areas not to be marbled were first painted out with masking fluid.

Above: Illustration for a magazine article on Michael Moorcock entitled 'Behold the Man', published by Paul Raymond. Acrylic gouache, crayon, ink and marbling.

Steve Ridgeway, art director of *Club International* commissioned this painting, which, though acknowledging Moorcock as a prolific author, contains elements which have no bearing at all on his work. The erotic teapot ('I'm a little teapot, small and stout . . .') has commercial possibilities, I feel sure.

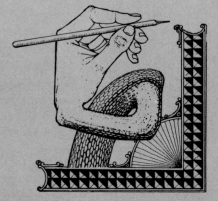

Above: Cover Art for *The Big Knockover* by Dashiell Hammett. (Ballantine—U.S.A.).

A symbolic treatment of the theme of gang warfare. Perhaps rather inappropriate for Hammett!

Section Eight:
BEASTS, MONSTERS AND HYBRIDS

Nothing delights me more than to invent new animal species, to exaggerate their characteristics, to combine them to make hybrids or chimerae. Fortunately, many of the commissions I have received, specifically requiring dragons, snakes or dinosaurs, have come close to the sort of pictures I should have been doing for myself anyway.

One of the main disadvantages of working for book jackets is that—unless the artist has an exceptionally fine technique—the artwork must be reduced before printing. Most of my paintings for book jackets are about twice the printed size, and, unless the printing is exceptionally good, do not benefit from reduction.

Another problem is the fact that the artist must allow space at the top of the picture (usually about one third of the area) for the art department to insert lettering. This is not done on the original artwork, so I do get the paintings back unmarked, but it does mean that the top third of all these pictures is virtually blank. For this reason I have cropped the top of most of those reproduced here.

Above: Cover Art for *One-Eye* by Stuart Gordon, published by Granada. Acrylic gouache and crayon.

Left: Cover Art for *Trullion, Alastor 2262* by Jack Vance, published by Granada. Acrylic gouache, crayon, ink and marbling.

Opposite page, top left: Cover Art for *Winter's Children* by Michael Coney, published by Sphere Books Ltd., London. Acrylic gouache, ink and crayon.

Opposite page, top right, Cover Art for *The Glass Key* by Dashiell Hammett. (Ballantine—U.S.A.). Acrylic gouache, ink, crayon and marbling.

Opposite page, lower left: Cover Art for *The Ice Schooner* by Michael Moorcock, published by Sphere Books Ltd., London. Acrylic gouache, crayon and ink.

Opposite page, lower right: Cover Art for *In the Kingdom of the Beasts* by Brian M. Stableford, published by Quartet Books Ltd., London. Acrylic gouache and ink.

Above: Cover Art for *Continuum One*, an anthology of science-fiction stories edited by Roger Ellwood and published by W. H. Allen Ltd., London. Acrylic gouache, crayon and ink.

Opposite page: Cover Art for *Continuum Two*, the sequel stories to the *Continuum One* anthology. Acrylic gouache, crayon and ink.

The four books in the series contained stories which continued from book to book—hence the title, so it was decided to treat the artwork in a similar way, so that, when displayed, the covers would look like one long painting.

The artwork for volumes two and three was in fact one painting. It was the intention that the main figure from each cover should appear in the background of the next.

Page 82, top: Cover Art for *Three Hearts and Three Lions* by Poul Anderson, published by Sphere Books Ltd., London. Acrylic gouache, crayon, ink and moss-size marbling.

Page 82, bottom: Cover Art for *The Half-Angels* by Andrew Lovesey, published by Sphere Books Ltd., London. Acrylic gouache, crayon, ink and marbling.

Page 83, top: Cover Art for *The Face in the Abyss* by A. Merritt, published by Futura Ltd., London. Acrylic gouache, crayon, ink and marbling.

Page 83, bottom: Cover Art for *Universe Five,* an anthology of science-fiction stories edited by Terry Carr and published by Popular Library, U.S.A. Acrylic gouache and crayon.

Pages 84 and 85: Cover Art for *Dwellers in the Mirage* by A. Merritt, published by Futura Ltd., London. Acrylic gouache, crayon, ink and marbling.

     Patrick Mortemore, art director at Futura, showed considerable professional courage when he used this potentially repugnant image to try to sell a book.

Above: Cover Art for *The Moon Pool* by A. Merritt. (Futura Ltd., London). Acrylic gouache, crayon, ink and moss-size marbling.

     'Moss-size' is probably the most difficult method of marbling—at least I have never been able to master it. The colours, which are water-based, are floated on a size (dilute glue) made from Irish moss, which is in fact a seaweed. The paper has to be treated so that it will absorb the colour, which stubbornly tends to sink into the size during the process. When many hours have already been spent on the drawing, this is a very risky process indeed, as the whole thing can be ruined.

86

Above: Cover Art for *The Face of Heaven* by Brian M. Stableford, published by Quartet Books Ltd., London. Acrylic gouache and crayon. (Reproduced by permission of Charles Haswell).

A rare attempt at restraint, at least as far as colour is concerned. At the time I was not aware that retailers generally consider green to be a slow-selling colour.

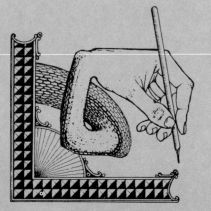

Above: Front Cover of *The Satyr's Head and Other Tales of Terror* edited by David A. Sutton, and published by Trans-world Ltd., London (Corgi). From an idea by Roger Hammond.

Acrylic gouache and ink. (Reproduced by permission of Howard Abramowitz).

Section Nine:
THE DEVIL

Satan seems to be coming into favour again. His face is certainly most picturesque, and his image appears to sell well these days.

Distortions, depravity and malevolence— horror has a surprising appeal. But a nightmare shared is a nightmare stilled. These images for me are nothing more than a visual game, a way of neutralising horror.

Above: Second Painting for the Cover of *Seven Footprints to Satan* by A. Merritt, published by Avon Books, U.S.A. Acrylic gouache, crayon, ink and marbling. (Front only).

I had already illustrated this book once (see pages 92-93) when Avon asked me to do something different for the American market. The sinister footprint in the stone is in fact my daughter Rosie's. I took a cast of her foot in Plaster of Paris.

Opposite: Cover Art for *Burn Witch Burn!* by A. Merritt, published by Futura Ltd., London. Acrylic gouache, crayon, ink and marbling. (Front only).

Pages 92 and 93: First Painting for the Cover of *Seven Footprints to Satan* by A. Merritt, published by Futura Ltd., London. Acrylic gouache, crayon, ink and marbling.

The 'Satan' in the book is a plunderer of art treasures as well as of men's souls. The octopoid creature is merely a symbolic representation of acquisitive evil, and does not appear in the narrative. I gave the book this treatment so that it would link up with *Dwellers in the Mirage* (see pages 84 and 85).

Section Ten:
DEATH

Death is even more popular than the Devil these days. Perhaps that is because in our modern lives of comfort and security, he is the only enemy we still all recognise, whatever our religious beliefs. We may no longer fear the Devil and the tortures of Hell, but Death is everywhere, the ultimate reward of all endeavour, the grinning bridegroom of both the wise and the foolish virgins.

Unfortunately for the artist there is only one universal death-symbol at his disposal: the skull. There are skulls everywhere on paperback book jackets. Surely it is time some original thinker came along with a symbol of sufficient power that would also be universally recognisable. In most cases my skulls were drawn 'from life' as it were, from a skull my father was given as a boy and which he passed on to me.

Above: First Painting for the Cover of *Red Harvest* by Dashiell Hammett. Acrylic gouache, crayon, ink and marbling.

Another inappropriately surrealistic treatment of a Hammett thriller.

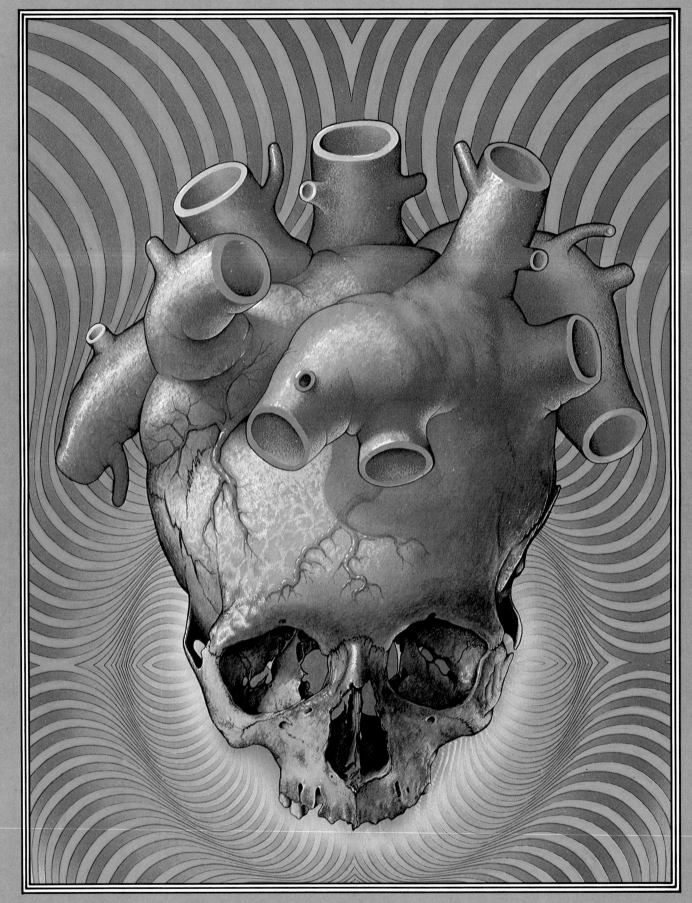

Above: *The Stagnation of the Heart.* One of two alternative ideas for the cover of a collection of stories entitled *Four for the Future,* edited by Harry Harrison, and published by Quartet Books Ltd., London. Acrylic gouache, crayon and ink.

The other alternative was 'Redemption' (see page 103), but the publishers rightly considered this painting more commercial. Apologies to Bridget Riley for blatantly plagiarising her optical effects in the background.

Above: Cover Art for *Line of Duty* by Ernest Tidyman, published by Transworld Ltd., London (Corgi). Acrylic gouache and ink.

Crooked cops. The protectors of society turn against it and abuse their authority.

Above: Cover Art for *Neq the Sword*, part three of Piers Anthony's trilogy, published by Transworld Ltd., London (Corgi). Acrylic gouache, crayon, ink and marbling.

This illustration is the third part of a single painting I did for all three books (see pages 105 and 110).

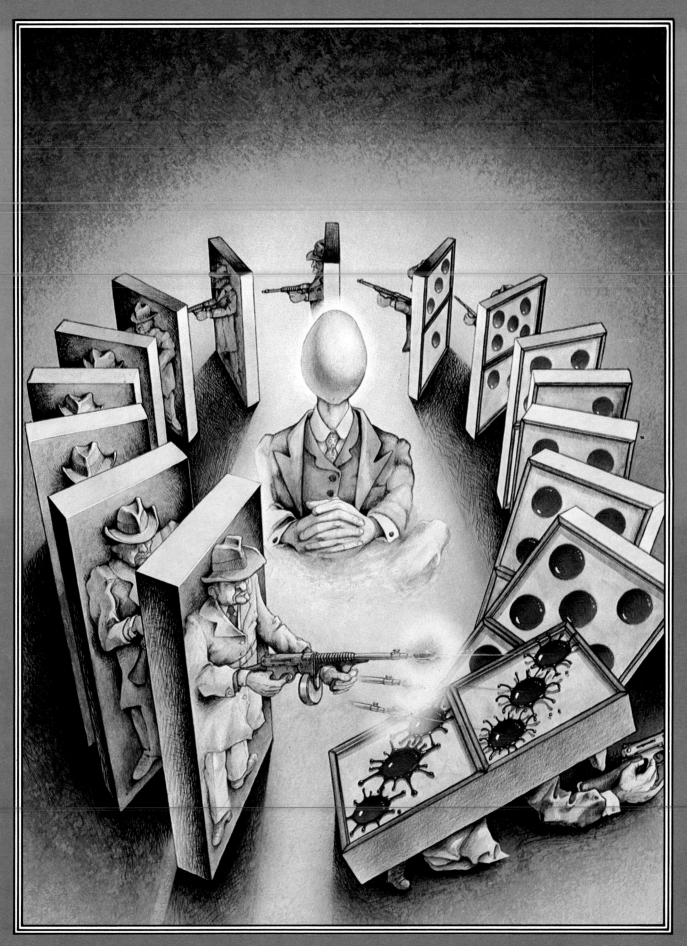

Above: Second Painting for the Cover of *Red Harvest* by
Dashiell Hammett. (Ballantine—U.S.A.). Acrylic gouache
and inks.

Closed-circuit revenge.

Pages 100 and 101: *The Graveyard* Cover Art for an anthology of ghost stories shortly to be published by Futura Ltd., London. Acrylic gouache.

Above: Second Painting for the cover of *Seven Footprints to Satan* by A. Merritt, published by Avon Books U.S.A. Acrylic gouache, crayon, ink and marbling. (Back).

Opposite: *Redemption.* The alternative design for the cover of *Four for the Future,* edited by Harry Harrison and published by Quartet Books Ltd., London (see page 96). Acrylic gouache, crayon and ink.

Apologies again to Bridget Riley. This idea was lifted bodily from the last drawing in the *Conflict* series (see page 9).

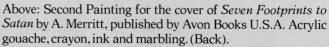

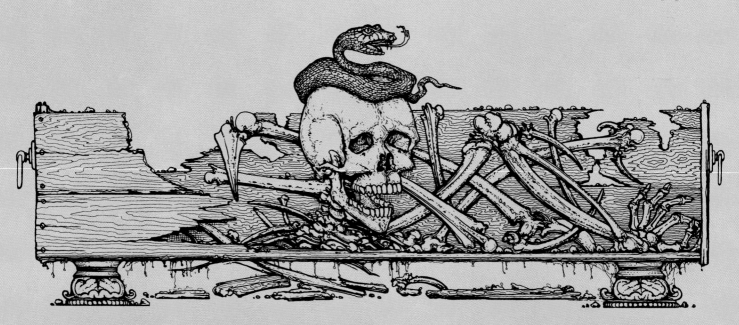

Above: Cover Art for *Var the Stick,* part two of Piers Anthony's extraordinary and convincing trilogy, published by Transworld Ltd., London (Corgi). (See also pages 98 and 110). Acrylic gouache, crayon, ink and marbling.

Section Eleven:
SUPER-HEROES

Piers Anthony's hypothetical post-nuclear society is surprisingly attractive. It is the super-hero's paradise. Like the knights errant of the Dark Ages, both the altruistic and the wicked perform their balletic aggressive displays. No groups are necessary, no societies can develop, for there is no lack of resources, no shortage of food or shelter; all this is provided by the intelligentsia, who live beneath the surface.

For me the originality of these books is that Piers Anthony understood — a rare thing in science-fiction literature, though Kurt Vonnegut has similar ideas — that the balmy, peaceful and secure Garden of Eden Utopia is in fact not very attractive to most people. After a day or two it would begin to pall, for most of us need excitement, stress, insecurity, even violence.

But this violence must be controlled, used for the benefit of the species, not to destroy it. When one male encounters another in Anthony's

Above left: Cover Art for *A Feast Unknown* by Philip José Farmer, published by Quartet Books Ltd., London. Acrylic gouache, crayon and ink.

I was very reluctant to illustrate this violent, and I believe, dangerous book. Indeed there was very little visual material in the text that could safely or decently be put on the cover.

Above right: Cover Art for *The Door into Summer* by Robert Heinlein, published by Pan Books Ltd., London. Acrylic gouache and ink.

By cryogenics to Utopia.

books, there is inevitably a ritualised battle, though always in single combat. These men are rutting stags enjoying their fight for the survival of the strong. Human society fits into the ecology like any other species; it cannot develop, cannot progress, cannot make the same mistakes again.

Like me, I believe that Piers Anthony half wishes that this dream could come true. Man once again the noblest of beasts, proud, strong and healthy. Yet this can surely never be enough; man is more than a beast, whether that extra ingredient that makes him so be good or bad,

helpful to the species or destructive of it. So these books are a holiday, a hypothesis. Anthony is simply saying: "What if . . .?", and that is, after all, the basis of all the best science-fiction, and of all the best surrealist painting.

Flabby and pale as we are, mere shadows of our noble and savage ancestors, we can still identify with our super-heroes, taste the thrills and freedoms that our over-technological and protected society cannot provide, content that within us we still hold the potential of rare breeds, the latent nobility of the happy savage.

Above: Cover Art for *Candy Man* by Vincent King, published by Sphere Books Ltd., London. Acrylic gouache, crayon, ink and marbling.

Another drama set in post-nuclear chaos. Do we all secretly look forward to the breakdown of society and the at least partial depopulation of the Earth?

Pages 108 and 109: Cover Art for *The Gray Prince* by Jack Vance, published by Avon Books U.S.A. Acrylic gouache, crayon and ink.

Above: Cover Art for *Sos the Rope*, part one of Piers Anthony's trilogy, published by Transworld Ltd., London (Corgi). Acrylic gouache, crayon, ink and marbling. (See also pages 98 and 105).

The best super-heroes, though strong and ruthless, usually have a subsidiary gentleness built in.

Opposite: Cover Art for *To Your Scattered Bodies Go* by Philip José Farmer, published by Granada Ltd., London. Acrylic gouache and crayon.

One of the best and most absorbing science-fiction stories I have ever read, though my cover does not do it justice. Richard Burton, the explorer, together with all humanity, past, present and future, finds himself reincarnated on 'Riverworld'.

On Page 112: Cover Art for *The Guns of Avalon* by Roger Zelazny, published by Transworld Ltd., London (Corgi). Acrylic gouache, crayon and ink.

The highly imaginative sequel to *Nine Princes in Amber.* (See page 135).

On Page 113: Cover Art for *The Seedbearers* by Peter Timlett, published by Transworld Ltd., London (Corgi). Acrylic gouache, crayon and ink.

The fall of Atlantis. The first volume of a remarkable trilogy which traces the refinement of religion and mysticism against a backcloth of savagery and excitement.

On Pages 114 and 115: Cover Art for *The Radio Planet* by
Ralph Milney-Farley, published by Ace Books U.S.A.
Acrylic gouache, crayon and ink.

The most recent book jacket painting reproduced in
this book.

Above: Cover Art for *Tales of Ten Worlds* by Arthur C. Clarke, published by Transworld Ltd., London. Acrylic gouache and ink.

Section Twelve:
THE UNIVERSE, SPACE-SHIPS AND FLYING MACHINES

Earth-bound we were, secure in this cradle-planet, but now we make our first tentative steps towards the stars. We can see it all, all the possible technology of the future, through the eyes of the science-fiction writers. How much of it will come true must remain for our children to see.

There are several illustrators in the field of space hardware—notably Chris Foss and Eddie Jones—whose gift is to convey the hugeness of their spacecraft, myriads of tiny details overlaid with the glowing mistiness of atmospheric perspective. But my space-ships always seem small and toy-like, more like models than the real thing. I also lack the knowledge of science and engineer-ing which would make them convincing. Anyway, here they are—conveyances our children may one day be using.

On Page 118: Cover Art for *Five Weeks in a Balloon* by Jules Verne, published by New English Library, London. Acrylic gouache, crayon and ink.

On Page 119: Cover Art for *The Warlord of the Air* by Michael Moorcock, published by Quartet Books Ltd., London. Acrylic gouache, crayon and ink.

Above: Cover Art for *Our Haunted Planet* by John A. Keel, published by Futura Ltd., London. Acrylic gouache and marbling.

Surely no one who saw those first photographs of the Earth seen from space can ever forget the profound change they made in our perspectives. Our attitudes are already less parochial, more cosmic. The old myths are no longer satisfying to us, who stand on the brink of a new inheritance.

Above: Cover Art for *The Forever War*, by Joe Haldeman, published by Futura Ltd., London. Acrylic gouache, ink, and black emulsion.

The conflicts and political division of earthbound civilization spread with us into space like a cancer, when we should treat it with respect, treading lightly as on virgin snow.

I drew these rather unlikely space-craft from models I had made from wood and plastic. It is strange how we still cling to the concepts of 'up' and 'down' when designing such machines. Surely these terrestrial attitudes will melt away once real ships are built for flight in deep space. But the illustrator is drawing for today's perspectives, and the book jacket must have a distintly 'right way up' look.

Above: Cover Art for *The Best of John Wyndham*, published by Sphere Books Ltd., London. Acrylic gouache, crayon, ink and marbling.

This was my first serious attempt at designing a space-craft. It was also the first cover I did after becoming the proud but inexperienced owner of an air-brush.

Up to now all my space-ships had been jokes (see *The Summerhouse* on page 19), whimsical adaptations of insects and buildings, and I found it hard to treat the subject in a serious manner, to give it the necessary grandeur and titanism. This ship looks as though it could be driven by a frog or a snail!

Above: Cover Art for *The Best of Robert Heinlein* published
by Sphere Books Ltd., London. Acrylic gouache, crayon,
ink and marbling.

Again an early attempt, this space-ship has a
Victorian look about it. Small and unconvincing, it would
look more at home in a children's book.

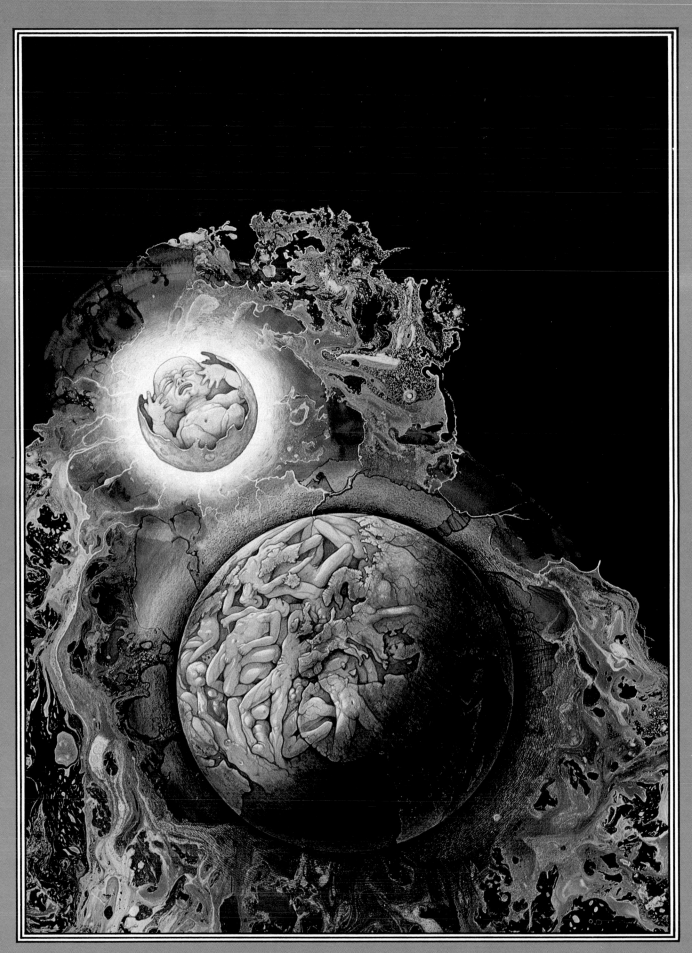

Above: Cover Art for *Day Million* by Frederik Pohl, published by Pan Books Ltd., London. Acrylic gouache, crayon, ink and marbling.

Above: Cover Art for *Day of Wrath* by Brian M. Stableford,
published by Quartet Books Ltd., London. Acrylic gouache,
crayon, ink and marbling.

On Page 126: Cover Art for *The Green Hills of Earth* by Robert Heinlein, published by Pan Books Ltd., London. Acrylic gouache, ink and marbling.

On Page 127: Cover Art for *The Book of Mars* edited by Jane Hipolit and Willis E. McNelly, and published by Futura Ltd., London. Acrylic gouache, ink and black emulsion.

On Pages 128 and 129: Cover Art for *New Worlds Eight* edited by Hilary Bailey, and published by Sphere Books Ltd., London. Acrylic gouache, ink and marbling. (Reproduced by permission of Charles Haswell).

On Pages 130 and 131: Cover Art for *Planet of the Blind* (left half) and *New Life for Old* (right half) by Laurence James, published by Sphere Books Ltd., London. Acrylic gouache.

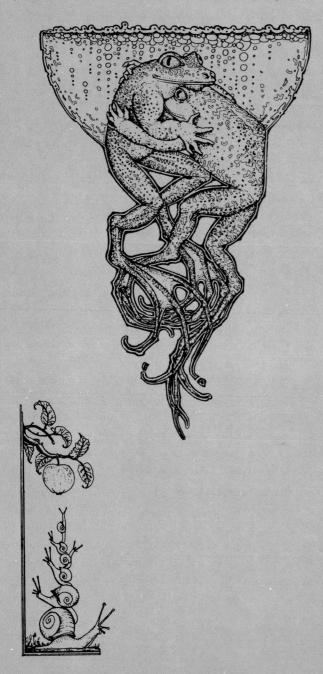

Section Thirteen:
SYMBOLS

As I said in the section on Death, there is a shortage of easily recognised symbols. Illustration of non-factual literature is perhaps the one field where symbolism really comes into its own. In many cases we draw on established vocabularies, but occasionally it is good to coin a new phrase.

Above: Cover Art for *The Billion Year Spree* by Brian Aldiss, a history of science-fiction published by Transworld Ltd., London (Corgi) October 1974. (Reproduced by permission of Kathryn Shelton-Jones).

An attempt to symbolise the passage of time, which not only brings to pass the visions of the prophets but also snuffs out the prophets themselves. The vision catches up with the visionary.

On Page 134: Cover Art for *Dangerous Visions* volumes one and two, edited by Harlan Ellison and published by Futura Ltd., London. May—June 1973. Acrylic gouache, crayon, ink and marbling.

A similar theme to that of *The Billion Year Spree.*

Above: Cover Art for *The Judgement of Eve* by Edgar Pangborn, published by Avon Books U.S.A. October 1975. Acrylic gouache and ink.

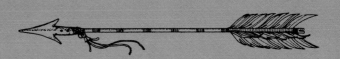

On Page 135: top left: *Nightfall,* Cover Art for *The Best of Isaac Asimov* published by Sphere Books Ltd., London. March 1973. Acrylic gouache and ink.

On Page 135, top right: Cover Art for *Nine Princes in Amber* by Roger Zelazny, published by Transworld Ltd., London. (Corgi) November 1973. Acrylic gouache and ink.

On Page 135, lower left: Cover Art for *The Thin Man* by Dashiell Hammett. (Ballantine—U.S.A.) February 1973. Acrylic gouache, crayon, ink and marbling.

On Page 135, lower right: Cover Art for *The Dain Curse* by Dashiell Hammett. (Ballantine—U.S.A.) February 1973. Acrylic gouache, crayon, ink and marbling.

Below left: Cover Art for *The New Adam* by Stanley G. Weinbaum, published by Sphere Books Ltd., London. August 1973. Acrylic gouache, crayon and ink.

Below right: Cover Art for *The Green Gene* by Peter Dickinson, published by Granada, London. December 1973. Acrylic gouache and ink.

Above: Cover Art for *A for Andromeda* and *Andromeda Break-through* by Fred Hoyle and John Elliott, published by Transworld Ltd., London (Corgi). April 1975. Acrylic gouache, crayon and ink.

The two books were designed to be displayed together so as to reconstruct the reels of a computer. (After an idea by Roger Hammond).

Below: Cover Art for *The Jargoon Pard* by Andre Norton, published by Victor Gollancz Ltd., London. January 1975. Acrylic gouache and crayon on a print from an etched copper plate.

A children's science-fiction publication. The mouth and the ear of course symbolise the story-teller and the listener.

Above: Cover Art for *A Song for Lya* by George R. R. Martin, published by Avon Books U.S.A. October 1975. Acrylic gouache and ink.

     Love gone insane.

Left: Cover Art for *Chamiel* by Edward Pearson, published by Quartet Books Ltd., London. June 1973. Acrylic gouache and ink.

On Page 138: Cover Art for *Waldo* by Robert Heinlein, published by Pan Books Ltd., London. (Front only). June 1974. Acrylic gouache, crayon, ink and marbling.

     The effete space-dweller dependent on prosthetic limbs.

On Page 139: Cover Art for *The Net* by Jean Renvoizé, published by Quartet Books Ltd., London. January 1974. Acrylic gouache and crayon.

     Frustrations of domesticity.

Above: Cover Art for *The Broken Sword* by Poul Anderson, published by Sphere Books Ltd., London. June 1973. Acrylic gouache, crayon and ink.

Right: Cover Art for *The Still Small Voice of Trumpets* by Lloyd Biggle Jr., published by Sphere Books Ltd., London. April 1975. Acrylic gouache, crayon, ink and marbling.

Above: Part of the Sleeve Painting for *Time and Tide,* an album by Greenslade on the Warner Brothers Label. Acrylic gouache, crayon and marbling. (Including the magician invented by Roger Dean).

Reproduced as a poster and as stickers, the original artwork unfortunately went 'missing' during production. An enlarged version of this painting was used as a backdrop during the band's performances.

Section Fourteen:
RECORD SLEEVES ETC.

It is difficult to break into this field, indeed there are very few artists who work exclusively for record sleeves.

My first record sleeve commission was from Ian Murray of Polydor, who asked me to dream something up for a new group called 'Ross'. All I had to go on was a tape recorded at the wrong speed for my machine. Anyway, I sent off a rough

Above: Sleeve Painting for *Ross* on RSO Records. January 1974. Acrylic gouache, crayon and ink. (In the collection of James Blyth).

sketch showing an assemblage of symbolic happenings around a female fortress figure. I later agreed to cut out a great deal of the incidental details so as to make a more immediate image, which was just as well, for in the event I had only three days in which to complete the final artwork!

PATRICK WOODROFFE 1974

Above: Cover Art for *The Marc Bolan Story* by George Tremlett, published by Futura Ltd., London. August 1974. Acrylic gouache, ink and marbling.

This is of course not a record sleeve, but I felt that it belonged in this section rather than in any other.

My original idea was to show the star of 'T Rex' as a tyrannosaurus singing into a microphone, but unfortunately the idea was considered a possible affront to the fans, so I had to think of something a little less whimsical. When exhibited in London, this painting provoked analysis by one reviewer who interpreted it as a symbolic comment on Bolan's at least temporary fall from glory and popularity, which was not at all what I intended.

Sketches for the paintings "Lovely Bird, will you stay and sing?"
and "While I Live, I shall...", for the sleeve designs for "Ross" and
Beethoven's "Emperor" Concerto.

Patrick Woodroffe September 1974.

What's this?
— an extreme coffee
pot, naturally.

BRASSO
VARDO

While I Live, I shall!
In the high wind I
shall flip!
In the surf my skin
shall turn!
And when I die I shall!
In the cold earth
My skin shall clothe snails.

WHILE
I LIVE
I SHALL

Rocks

Strong and Valiant
the noble knight,
FORTINBRASSO

And God spoke to me by
the cliffs, and said,
"Raise your rocks to you,
and mine to me!"

I looked at
the foot
of the
rock

CONCENTRIC
SPECTRUM
COLOURS

BRASSO
PROFUNDO

EX BRASSO BONGO

As I drew by the
cliffs, the old woman
and old women
approach. "Is there a
path?" they ask me
Another, but turn away
and go. There was a path,
and now they'll never know.

A strange exchange
gives us the costume
and the hare-man.
Who says horses
songy battles? But
then fight to gain
their true shapes.

Oats eat catmeat, dogs
eat dogmeat. But horses
don't like horsemeat,
dogs don't eat pigmeat.
What meat do you
eat?

Snails have ears — as
distinct you know! And
And snails are comp-
osers too! They write
grimplodding marches

CHESTER
WHITE SOW.

But and Beethoven
have much more
in common than
mammary glands.

VANISHING
BONE

Above: Sleeve Painting for Beethoven's 'Emperor' Concerto.
March 1974. Oil on wood. (Reproduced by permission of
CBS Records Ltd., London).

When Roslav Szaybo, art director at CBS Records, commissioned a painting to be used on the sleeve of a recording of Beethoven's 'Emperor' Concerto, he specified that it should be in oils, and in the style of *Hunting Party at the World's End*. (See page 18). So I assembled a number of symbols which I thought appropriate, and also allowed one or two of my own to stray in. The painting was accepted by CBS, but has not been used on a sleeve to date.

This brief excursion back into my own personal mythical kingdom provoked a period of dissatisfaction with the commercialism of my recent work. So I took several months off all commissioned work and produced a number of paintings and sketches purely for my own amusement. Many of the three-dimensional objects in Section Six were done during this period. But the tension brought about by the knowledge that I was earning no money at all soon made me accept

Above: Sleeve Painting for *Greenslade (2)*. November 1975.
Acrylic gouache, crayon and ink.
   The lettering was left unfinished, as no title had yet
been given to the album.

commissions again. Indeed I was glad to get back
to the routine, so conditioned had I become to the
urgency of deadlines and the specific requirements
of art directors.

   Andrew McCulloch, the drummer with
'Greenslade', was so pleased with the first painting
which I did for *Time and Tide,* that I was asked
straight away to commit myself to producing the
artwork for their next album. Unfortunately when
the time came the group ran into various problems
and the album never came out.

Above: Sleeve Painting for the album *Bandolier* by 'Budgie'.
July 1975. Acrylic gouache and crayon. (Reproduced by
permission of MCA Records Ltd.).

Graham Maloney, manager of 'Budgie', took
a trip to Cornwall to discuss the artwork for this
sleeve, though the art direction was by John Pasche
of Gull Graphics.

The brief which I received seemed impossible. I was to base the sleeve on 'Planet of the
Apes', but instead of apes' heads, I was to use
budgerigars' heads. The budgies were also required
to look 'fierce'. So here it is: 'Planet of the Budgies'.

It is unfortunate that there is so little work
available in this field, for I prefer working for
record sleeves, mainly because of the format,
which allows one to work same size, thus obviating
the need for reduction. It is also refreshing not to be
obliged to leave a great deal of space at the top
for lettering.

One also comes into contact with the people
producing the music. 'Judas Priest' and 'Greenslade' have been particularly appreciative, whereas
you rarely meet or even hear from the authors of
paperbacks. It is also good to see a record's position
in the charts, whereas science-fiction paperbacks
very rarely make the best-seller lists.

Above: Sleeve Painting for *Sad Wings Of Destiny* by 'Judas Priest'. January 1976. Acrylic gouache, crayon, ink, and marbling. (Reproduced by permission of Gull Records Ltd.). My most recent record sleeve painting.

Above: Detail from the triptych: THE THOUSAND-YEAR
ROUNDABOUT. The windows of Hell.

EPILOGUE

So our life is a walk down a corridor whose
walls are pasted with images. We are dazzled by
the visions that assault our senses, we try to make
sense of them, and when we fail we comfort ourselves by turning our vision inwards. These are
personal myths, our surreal adventures in
nowhere-land.

Above: WITHIN THE WICKER FENCE. Oil on wood.
May 1974.

We are borne along by the stream of life,
bounded by fictional wicker fences we have
erected ourselves, guided by guardian angels
whose motives we know not; are they benign or
malignant, these protectors of our fenced domains?
For the eyes of birds are inscrutable. Our only
escape is by fantasy, a tree springing into the
depths of the sky, though its roots are imprisoned
in the soil on which it depends for life.

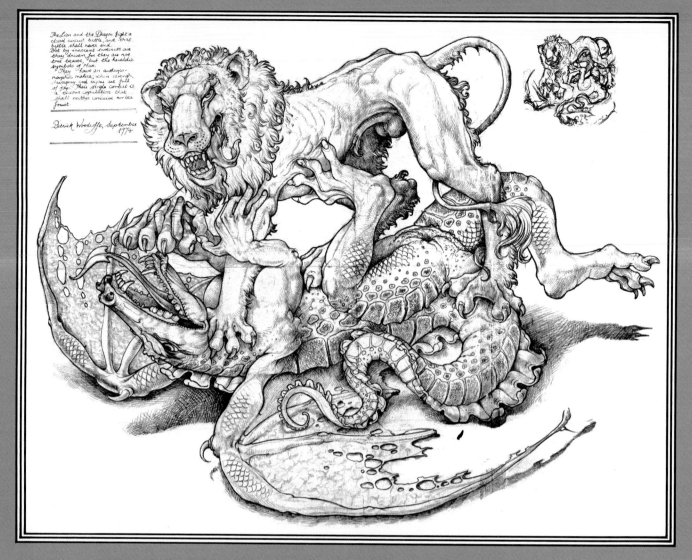

Above: THE LION AND THE DRAGON. Pencil. September 1974.

We must resist the temptation to bring our fantasies to life and impose them on others, for they surely have their own. The lion has a vision of a world free of dragons, and the dragon sees a world empty of lions. Their battle is savage and cruel, but though they tear their heads from their bodies, their war will still continue, for like the hydra of Lerna, new heads spring up from the roots of the old.

Let it be—what can never be. Fold away your talons and your claws, learn to live in harmony and peace. May Utopia remain a dream, Erewhon forever Nowhere. For what is truth? Only a flickering of images in our brains. And what is fiction? Nothing more nor less than truth, save that we may keep it to ourselves.

154

And when you have finished your little flight around the park, you who would have walked around the world, bequeath to your children your myths and your fantasies, that the richness of human experience may become a book for all to read, a testament from the dying eye, a picture of the inside of the dying brain, a Mythopœikon

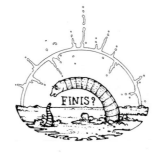

Sincere thanks to Carla Capalbo and Jim Slattery
for their invaluable help in the preparation of the
text for this book.

P. W. July 1976.

The children's book *Micky's New Home,*
with text and illustrations by Patrick Woodroffe,
is also published by Dragon's Dream.